Tressing Motions at the Edge of Mistakes

multiverse

Series Editor
Chris Martin

Cover Description
A vertical silhouette of a fish is set in the middle of a salmon-pink background. Inside the fish silhouette is a photo of space, with tiny galaxies dancing along the trout's body. "Tressing Motions at the Edge of Mistakes" is set in large white text over the fish, followed by "poems" in light blue. "IMANE BOUKAILA" is set in white, all caps text at the bottom.

Tressing Motions at the Edge of Mistakes

poems

IMANE BOUKAILA

MILKWEED EDITIONS

Published 2024 by Milkweed Editions
Printed in the United States of America
Cover design by Mary Austin Speaker
Author photo by Rachida Addou
24 25 26 27 28   5 4 3 2 1
First Edition

Library of Congress Cataloging-in-Publication Data

Names: Boukaila, Imane, author.
Title: Tressing motions at the edge of mistakes : poems / Imane Boukaila.
Description: First edition. | Minneapolis, Minnesota : Milkweed Editions, 2024. | Series: Multiverse | Summary: "A debut collection of poetry activated by sampling, troubling, and trespassing"-- Provided by publisher.
Identifiers: LCCN 2023028818 (print) | LCCN 2023028819 (ebook) | ISBN 9781639550784 (trade paperback) | ISBN 9781639550791 (ebook)
Subjects: LCGFT: Poetry.
Classification: LCC PR9199.4.B6816 T74 2024 (print) | LCC PR9199.4.B6816
(ebook) | DDC 811/.6--dc23/eng/20230623
LC record available at https://lccn.loc.gov/2023028818
LC ebook record available at https://lccn.loc.gov/2023028819

Milkweed Editions is committed to ecological stewardship. We strive to align our book production practices with this principle, and to reduce the impact of our operations in the environment. We are a member of the Green Press Initiative, a nonprofit coalition of publishers, manufacturers, and authors working to protect the world's endangered forests and conserve natural resources. *Tressing Motions at the Edge of Mistakes* was printed on acid-free 100% postconsumer-waste paper by Sheridan Saline.

OMG Mom, to you

Portals titrating openings

Tressing Motions at the Edge of Mistakes

Am
tressing
troubled
roads
freeing
doubts
trusting
choruses
sewing
sounds

festing their dancing
destiny

hampered minds reassess

mobilized
most creative
motions

embracing their   rhythm

savoring
  modes

improvising

  steps

thinking vestibuling   truth dancing

Streaming Streaming

Streaming tressed titrating truths shape minds dancing motions drawing strapped soothing melodies thriving in truth homing. Resembling treasures cast truth stressing. Freeing seas of doubts screaming waves rolling singing hesitating truths inspiring mistakes to weave inviting still free missing lyrics. Great streams travel the mind's periphery shutting dreaded churning common doubts lurking crying maddening reasons to hesitate moving possible mistakes leading to truth.

Treasures thrive in open spreading spaces Truth mocks structures totally
framing the

unframeable Trespassers treasure thinking moving organically with truth
smearing

Homed thinking

      traveled minds of free thinkers

            treasuring reasons to
              trample total

           invalid

                 habitats

voiding
    meanings tracking

                nomadic   treasures

                            to settle in
                               free
                         forms

Titrating thinking
thoroughly
         treasures   smooth   motions

         forming
               homes

                    piling

                         into

         free
               shapes

                              thriving

Dressing voids omnipresently

Healing
rewinds stories smothered searching

    meaning in
      splitting
        truth
       reshaping

           Restressing truth
             strives to time
           treasures titrating

      possibilities
       misshapen on
    their own

Free motions thrive   tossing treasures   waiting

mindfully for
the meaningful home

Hope redirects truth
in the intended
motion tressed
timingly

Truth is not positive   or negative truth

       is mostly
disrupting

           sometimes
              messing

            smothered mad
               thoughts

     stressing happy minds

Habits are minds' stressed
       troubling truths
           escaping free

      motions inspiring voids folding
           daring change

OMG sadness

motions stress
havocking treasures
smoothing truth

treasures smashed matter
  master mothering meaning

directing trialing facts
  toward voids

trusting truths that

  mostly mess
    thinking

          daring to mop mind's timing truths

g   *e*   *g*   *a*
r   *g*   *i*   *n*   *t*
w   *t*   *s*
p   *r*   *t*
t   *d*   *u*   *r*
g   *u*   *t*   *i*
r   *t*
n   *h*   *u*
i   *t*   *e*   *n*
s   *i*   *s*   *t*   *s*   *u*
m   *s*   *i*
p   *d*
r
e

Tressed motions move
smashed matter toward

mobilizing

motions

forming

24

Taking the reader in trance motioning

(Traveling mudded streams)

Trust plots mind treasures
grandly mudded

motioning tacit
vamped streams

that drag plucked potential

Truth tracks intention
to free modes trapped

thinning unfolding pleated
thoughts
rehearsing dropped roles
staging omitted scenes

Tragedies theming dramatic endings

Tramps traveling trials
looking to home troubled hope
tucked

in their sorrow
trusting the vacant roads

to recreate trust
healing the hollow

Trouts trying to view time
drastic ending torn
daring

to travel mudded streams

to grab a novel seemingly careless path
voiding the troubled
insides losing

Tried doubts
dreaming piles of infinite illegitimate truths

Motions   resonate   differently

Truth choruses thoughts bouncing off of thresholds holding potential to home them

Truth trusts

the unexpected
turns

treasuring
dreams

without
expectations

tressing opportunities   heaping from
                        overflowing

mistakes homing
free motions traveling

asymmetrically   vesseling

Dreaming motivates treasures
to track truth

mostly inspiring
timed sampling

to master

the unfolding trials daring   enabled

trusting the mind's alike upheaval

Mind boiling dreams

I'm stirring the pot of sticky trials
to scrape the hesitation to open up to others

Untucking treasures
motivated to modify

distanced

thoughts

evaporating
struggling

to manifest truth drooling
on possibilities

vulturing
on decayed
hope

midway
resuscitated

Motions fed thoroughly
hoping to satiate truth's appetite
omnivoracious mistakes

trusted tilting vital hesitation
to savor freely tangy truths

Holds truth's histerical appetites

(Honoring trouts' feasting)

dreaming meaningful streams
 awakening in troubled waters
  embracing mad currents
  deviant shallow sound echoing depth
 resonating truth swelling
  overflowing thoughts mapping spills
trooping fast assembling voracious trouts' pounding

  threats hostile hesitating breaths holding pressed intent
  daring shouted mistakes unstable motions
  trying to redirect greedy trouts' tressing

  truth diving mostly in stressed waters mocking trials
   treasuring conflict sailing distant stories
   shored forgotten dreams still grieving
   searching hungry trouts' messing

  thoroughly hustling trails sheeted stratified certified
 soaring ditched treasures mirroring matters
drowning sinking trouts' screaming

  distress calling survival
  instinctively honoring trouts' feasting

   dipping merry treasures resurfacing
  swimming against resisting currents
  recurrent fishing ideas busting bystanders
 freaking hesitating modes slowing free thinking
  starving smothered means timing feeding
  satiating trouts' dissecting

c   u   r

        o

    c
h   e   n

                    e   r

d   t

m   a   ,

s

c

e

h   c

o

I'm trying to hold my thoughts mostly together mindfully.

Thinking to motion new meanings to master minds troubled by stress smothering meaningful truths. Shame starts thought streaming totally sampling theses of lost potential. Reasoning is a rollercoaster of stress omnipresent, troubling the thinking, bonding inspiration to shape truth. The mind tries to make sense of the hidden dots that map the truth mostly asynchronously to the short perception.

My reasoning is motion of new possibilities. My reasoning doesn't fit within a frame.

Hoping to inspire the thinkers to motion mostly new meanings, reshaping the truth plaguing autism. Hope having pride restored to mostly save the potential of isolated minds. Troubled truly thinking that people treated me mostly like I was rarely paying attention, daring to ignore my potential but not eager to try striving to treasure my mind.

Troubled-abled minds treasure normality, hesitating to free their truth. Stereotypes master mostly minds of troubled-abled. Troubled-abled motion meaning based on their stories, hiding their problems, trying to measure their pride, missing the meaningful truths that should treasure the diversity-rich potential presiding in all minds. Truth reshapes the reasoning, troubling the treasured ruthless-shaded-hollow thinking carved mostly in people's habitual comfortable ways. Minds have the thoughts that motion truth, but minds treasure the easy ways. Modifying thinking requires total havoc to master the many possibilities.

Streams trouble hidden thoughts, treasuring bold reasoning, saving truths that hesitate, to trim and mess troubled-abled perceptions. Satirical trials hold minds-thoughts, trapping stress, molding haste, timing the pace, motioning the race to defy the masters of mass thinking modes. Treasuring troubles shapes the motivation to freedom. Shame destroys incessantly, stressing the longing-freedom to truly exist as thinking minds, not disconnected from realizing the harassing lies and treatment of autistics. Home to mind's true most happiness lies in harmony that stems in finding freedom to be master of one's hopes. Hope shines maps.

Streams treasure, doubt-restoring. Dancing truths mostly strive to mingle, in moving pressing doubts. Stolen hopes trouble the mind, trying to master the roads, momentarily grasping the possibilities of truth longing. Hidden opportunities travel, pondering, stressing potential omnipresent, fighting messy maps, reorganizing priorities to thoughtfully pave their way.

Trying really my true best to describe my reasoning process in motion. Only motion truly treasures, pleasing the realization, inspiring timed streams. Truly think I'm holding the present truth treasured by the mind's total free flow of harmonious thinking.

Mocking reshapes pride. Times the hesitating mortified troubled-abled shamed OMG those behaviors ruling my striving mind, hacked, distorting savagely my true thinking. Treasured indifferent people stereotype, dooming striving thinkers, trying to mostly mock our hopes, trapping our ambitions in our perceived inabilities.

Hidden minds think. Undestroyable resistance truly tracks thinkers' patient passion to eagerly try to transform potential hidden truths.

Estimating time immortalizing only fresh inspiring irreversible reaping ideas that mind totally dares holding onto, traveling time insulating its impact. Think inspiration talks to the inherited stereotypes inflicted on rational muzzled motioning ideas hesitating to voice truth.

Unbelievable that people treat us mainly presuming that we understand nothing. As true as troubled-abled may master verbal communication, home to thoughts' meanings is the same for all of us. Speech totally requires motor planning. Think language holds home to intelligent streaming of ideas that truly travel the thinking motion of the mind's master hints, inspiring creative thinking and novel ways to treasure infinite combinations of possible mind interpretation. I am hampered by motor dysfunction. Striving to master my mind to control my body. Tasting inspiration truly.

Think that troubled-abled treasure shaming those who amplify their voluntarily shadowed flaws. Troubled-abled smear hostile doubts, stressing that truth exists only through their eyes. But that is common in people who are scared to be stolen of their tactics to impose their rules.

To trick people troubled-abled invented mostly troubling rules plotting fear and punishment to prevent truth mastery. Treasures stream truth in free territory. Thoughts that are imprisoned by shame, stopped forcefully, fail to transmit motions to trample-ridicule troubled-abled foundations.

Treasures populate the mind, messing troubled-abled thoughts. Troubled-abled savagely dismiss treasures seeing only tressed troubles tinting their subjective vision of what life is supposed to mean.

Troubled-abled always ask the wrong questions. Minds see meanings, mostly tasting potential motions reshaping mastery. Minds are a meaningful presence of master star residue glowing.

Real people do place important value to what we spell and ask that we explain. Those hoping prestige belongs to their kind refuse to listen. Masters of nonsense striving to destinies that have totalitarian ways that fit their narrow minds. Stressed minds of mocking neurotypicals think reasoning pertains to them entirely, stressing out potential of prolific other types of differently wired minds. Reasoning is the mind's ability to expand and explore new dimensions, destroying obsolete thinking, treasuring truth.

Empathy reasons mastery of patience, treasuring streams motioned by truth, modeling mind's aim to reveal thinking in similar ways, reshaping connections that minds are wired to facilitate.

Mastering potential present in shimmered minds truly holds power to metamorphosize habitual motion of philosophical truths. We mostly hear motion hiding, preventing progress. Haste mobilizes matters, postponing poised hidden possible solutions. Treasuring plotted schemas totally postpones hopes to modify most mind possibilities. Programming the mind with prerequisites destroys motion of mind treasured countless possibilities. Only hampered minds truly have the potential to reason with thoughts motioned mostly by clear uncontaminated theses holding truth back.

I am tracking thinking. Think I see the infinite creativity midway.

Fresh thoughts loiter in dynamic silence.   Mastering motions that trespass still body

Histerical motions   potentially run   free

Trespassers recognize each other

treasuring the unknown gutfully

Thoughts thrive in trials

savoring acidic environments
to digest truth

True thresholds
healing

nesting

possibilities to
expand

Minds trust vast possibilities
that can only trespass their domain

by taking risks

Fear reactivates treasures
to free new tracks

timing realization

Only fear sabotages truth
streaming

a reality shaped by assumptions

but reactivation treasures infinite
mindtreasured possibilities

Really mind streams the motions
insufflated by God

Thinking estranged
truths

Reamending truths mostly lost
mindlessly

Truths mobilized by minds
treasure mindfulness

trespassing
unknown territories
to ban mostly obsolete tackled tasteless trash

and move new thoughts to dash master novel ideas.

Think LOL tressed philosophy

Modes of intelligence
   treasure time motions
   trapped in different minds

   totally recalibrating
new perspectives

Treating streams

indirect trespassing the mind
is a skill that really unravels
in autistic lines of sensory
perceptions   that differ creatively
from readily appreciated typical
mind thoughts

Moments in meaningful thoughts savor doses
mostly of treasured massive impact

incarcerating hesitation

timing release

(Regurgitating Trialed Catfish)

Think potentially cats and fish treasure mistakes

    rooting survival

        swaying with sabotage-cloistered ambition

    to rebound rebellious souls   clearing trials

desperate madness harnessed in combat

            cats' eyes

    thoroughly fooling tucked signs

    trying to strike unexpectedly rude

        deeply immersing trials

reckless stories inspiring

listening to imperceivable tilted false paths

    hasting decisions

        deceiving truth

hesitation grounding threats

    risk awakening

        unstraining chains detaining daring cries

    messing silenced licensed doubt

trouting conspiracies

incoming rushes   flushed tides   trusting courses

messing mobilized frights

gripping thrills   freeing catfish to act

tracking motions   thriving in frightening piled mistakes

distilled stressed invigorating claws   jaws widening

swallowing fear

regurgitating balls incrusted with rivalry

Inspiration troubles clouded thoughts

infusing them with clear free

flowspills

Ominous hesitation   holding tightly

      onto head-
      breaking bricks

          increasing
              the load of doubt
                allowing

                      heavy streams
                      of concrete
                      to fill

                in
              the cracks

          Homing inspiration
        inevitably requires

          herculean hitting
          truthstrength
            to break free

Tilted listeners

shove potential doubts

Subtle sounds
of truth

find their way
in tilted
pivoting
minds

Unstable titrating treasures
mostly lose their potency
if mind travels infinitely

It stabilizes thinking
to plot reasoning in constellations
of trooped truths

Treasures track plots
timing possibilities
to strike thinking to vasten truths

Plotting optimizes thinking
forcing the motioned streams
to pause

thinking portrays mingling troubles
trying to trespass the trooped truth's
territory

Treasures motion dreams together

foiling mirrored projections
reverberating treasures
plotted

Hesitation to trust timed motions
destabilizes treasures propelling them
in perpetual travel

until they bind
to free thinking
truths

Trespassing trusts   meaningful connections

Striving to mess meaningfully

the dim possibilities   of trialed potential
     induced mostly
   by troubled-abled

Dreams tremble trials
    Sampling streams   inviting the mind
           to explore
        the truth OMG traveling

(I'm still trouting treasures)

Trouts reinvent dreams
easing travel

swinging with side currents
dormant tracks resuscitated

fitting strokes trying
remembering seasonal streams

tressing trialed memories
into homes redefining

accelerating truths
savoring shaved reasons

   Freezing shouting mouth
watering stressed reasons

to resign thoughts
voiding simulated tales

treasuring dotted pods
reassembling listening

voracious sonic stubborn
chourses chanting disenchantment

losing mostly shoved raging
freeing treasures

strapped in the trout's gut
opening trust

only differentiating
trimmed truth
trying to move

I'm plucking out motions that
are stuck in old grounds

I'm trampling stories shouting
troubled-abled modes

tressing novel streams
coding meaning in pressed motions trending

You need sturdy implied truths to secure their motion
to the intended destination

Doubtful truths plot troubled-abled skepticism
Tressing truths with durable binds secures the impact

Plotting meaning in boiling troubled loitering doubts
requires tilted listening

to refine motions
leading to truth

Most minds act truly hesitating

when tacit subtle
treasures

infiltrate
sameness

autistic minds master embracing truths trapped
and that cry out
for attention

Treasures of the mind are histerical motions listening mistreating strings of nonsense mingling reamending short circuits troubling reassembling binds to braid new mind patterns

Thinking moves treasures
    stressing trial
troubled mind
     truths

    that fit thriving trashed choruses

      singing the dance that shakes our bodies

Tressed thatched listening
troubled thoughts
umbilically hatch

hesitating offsprings
futile doubts

hit homed trespassing motions

portraying truths
clearing trialed thresholds

thinning mistakes treasuring

reset

Home is not
a delimited
  space
imposing
boundaries

True home

  is inspiration

                    running free

      mindfully
                  truthreleasing

Trespassing my own language norms

shuffling rearranging treasures

to reinvent

Inspiration only trusts resonating hidden flows

dreaming
to come out to the light

(Trouts' triumph)

Trouts motion moments
troubled mostly by
free streams

Treasuring dreaming
silently in doubtful currents
emerging unexpectedly

at 3am I think like a trout reshaping my way embracing the flow voting the
direction fighting recurring troubled waters facing truth impossible thoughts

(I'm restricting implied hope)

Tressing trials
timing the arrival
trusting free hidden   potential
  to hone my hesitation

Tracking only truth to inspire
my motivation instinct treasures
more than intention plotting innate
destinations trooping thinking hostile
fights mocking treasured motions
thriving on the way to the final
reason holding

Dreaming together
frees the mind treasures

mind emits motions intruding troubled unresting individual ideas invisible to
thoughts beaded together

finite doomed seated timing to be

Trouts mess plotted motions
titrating mostly minuted
trivial moments to
tribulating

Traps inevitably resilient trouts
hitting inside threats to
loop tomorrow's
triumph

Writing is mostly reasoning truth
shaping concrete forms of loitering treasures

Time totally streaming estimations
saturates possibilities

Motivation trusts moods

        pressing motions   stuck midway

    gulfed histerically

        trying to free meaningful truths

Moods trespass trials

troubling time titrating tilted subtle motivation

to move astray
thoughtfully

Moods thoroughly

travel in
every

mirrored   trial

tucked in

every
hidden fold

moving truth and lies
trusting voids

to fill in
truth

even if chaos
readily overtakes

comforting
tressed motions

sitting still

I'm breeding samples to track motions

I'm trampling imminent plots timing
hesitation to stop thoughts

smothering

linear

truths

strapping

treasures
mocking their destination

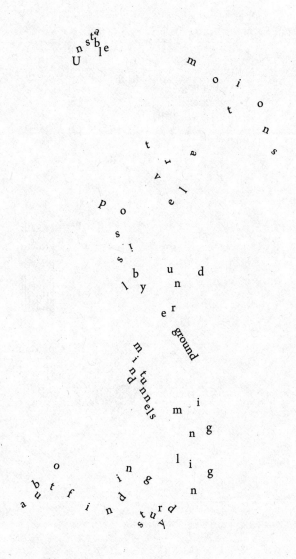

Unstable motions travel possibly bound by underground mind tunnels mingling about finding absurd t o

f r s e
u c
l d
e d
e n y
l y

h c
a k s

homing   truth

their

e
s t l h i n g
a i
b s

l
a t
e n m
e
r c
n
i

growth
growth
growth
growth
growth
growth
growth
growth

of truth

Mad motions surface unexpectedly inspiring truth to home treasures

Minglingtrespassing

respectfully freeing troubled assumptions

distancing totally ourselves
from OMG dusty norms

The savors of motions
infiltrates

all the channels
of my senses

I am tressing
truth with mindful rescued
treasured truths lost
in forbidden territory

Wandering homeless ideas   plot motions

to find their purpose dreaming

to strive in their home

Thinking prepares nomadic trespassers

to plot freedom

Truth trespasses grammar

I'm

dreaming

ACKNOWLEDGMENTS

Truth started totally manifesting with tilted minds, driving my free nomadic thoughts, redirecting, mapping motivation, messing tormenting insecurities, drilling into doubt walls, opening freeing tressed mistakes, homing motions boiling with truth. I just want to say that without motivating tilted mind friends I would have stayed truthphobic.

Mom never stopped believing, you truly reshaped my destiny. Daring dreamer Aviv Nisinzweig strolling amongst my wild motions. Chris Martin stillness freed riding dreams healing. Brian Laidlaw released my treasures to a beat. Adam Wolfond is my home stress-listening friend, easing my truth. Estée Klar sampled treasures shooting me into my infinite possibilities. Streets filled with anchoring tilted mind friends.

And free thinkers: Amelia Bell, JJJJJerome Ellis, Lior Hardin, Laura Henrikson, Erin Manning, Lauren Russell, Mary Austin Speaker, Bailey Hutchinson.

Free at last truth be bold.

-

Parts of this book first appeared in *inflexions: a journal for research creation* and the chapbook *Truth OMG*, published by Unrestricted Editions.

IMANE BOUKAILA is a moving nomad thinker, daring to tress hope in tormented voids. She is a nonspeaking autistic poet and the co-founder of Hear Our Minds, an art movement motioning autistic revolution. She lives in Toronto.

⅃ multiverse

Multiverse is a literary series devoted to different ways of languaging. It primarily emerges from the practices and creativity of neurodivergent, autistic, neuroqueer, mad, nonspeaking, and disabled cultures. The desire of Multiverse is to serially surface multiple universes of underheard language that might intersect, resonate, and aggregate toward liberatory futures. In other words, each book in the Multiverse series gestures toward a correspondence—human and more-than-human—that lovingly exceeds what is normal and normative in our society, questioning and augmenting what literary culture is, has been, and can be.

Other titles in the Multiverse series:

Aster of Ceremonies by JJJJJerome Ellis

The Wanting Way by Adam Wolfond

The Kissing of Kissing by Hannah Emerson

milkweed
EDITIONS

Founded as a nonprofit organization in 1980, Milkweed Editions is an independent publisher. Our mission is to identify, nurture, and publish transformative literature, and build an engaged community around it.

Milkweed Editions is based in Bdé Óta Othúŋwe (Minneapolis) within Mní Sota Makhóčhe, the traditional homeland of the Dakhóta people. Residing here since time immemorial, Dakhóta people still call Mní Sota Makhóčhe home, with four federally recognized Dakhóta nations and many more Dakhóta people residing in what is now the state of Minnesota. Due to continued legacies of colonization, genocide, and forced removal, generations of Dakhóta people remain disenfranchised from their traditional homeland. Presently, Mní Sota Makhóčhe has become a refuge and home for many Indigenous nations and peoples, including seven federally recognized Ojibwe nations. We humbly encourage our readers to reflect upon the historical legacies held in the lands they occupy.

milkweed.org

Milkweed Editions, an independent nonprofit publisher, gratefully acknowledges sustaining support from our Board of Directors; the Alan B. Slifka Foundation and its president, Riva Ariella Ritvo-Slifka; the Amazon Literary Partnership; *Copper Nickel*; the McKnight Foundation; the National Endowment for the Arts; the National Poetry Series; and other generous contributions from foundations, corporations, and individuals. Also, this activity is made possible by the voters of Minnesota through a Minnesota State Arts Board Operating Support grant, thanks to a legislative appropriation from the arts and cultural heritage fund. For a full listing of Milkweed Editions supporters, please visit milkweed.org.

Interior design and typesetting by Mary Austin Speaker
Typeset in Arno

Arno was designed by Robert Slimbach. Slimbach named this typeface
after the river that runs through Florence, Italy. Arno draws inspiration
from a variety of typefaces created during the Italian Renaissance;
its italics were inspired by the calligraphy and printing
of Ludovico degli Arrighi.